Original Flamboyance

Original Flamboyance

poems by
Anita Sullivan

SHANTI ARTS PUBLISHING
BRUNSWICK, MAINE

Original Flamboyance

Copyright © 2022 Anita Sullivan

All Rights Reserved
No part of this document may be reproduced or transmitted in any form or by any means without prior written permission of the publisher, except in the case of brief quotations embodied in critical reviews.

Published by Shanti Arts Publishing

Designed by Shanti Arts Designs

Cover image by Tim Sullivan and used with his permission

Shanti Arts LLC
193 Hillside Road
Brunswick, Maine 04011
shantiarts.com

Printed in the United States of America

ISBN: 978-1-956056-48-8 (print; softcover)

Library of Congress Control Number: 2022947289

Judicare vivos et mortuos

There is a breach in the wall between the living and the dead, a doorway
without a door.

A hinge hangs above this gap like the lid over a frog's eye,
indicating a necessity to pause, while the air thins to transparency.

Now in late November as I sit on the marble bench by the willow tree
gazing down at its last leaves heaped around an empty clay pot

I feel myself transforming into a gargoyle. This is a landscape for one
who has lived but lives not now, a large category of beings.

Or I might have said: this is a landscape for one who has never been alive,
and still lives not, but may yet do so, a large category of beings.

I look at the ground with its layered fragments, and recognize an entire middle realm.
Here you may place your finger upon the hidden tongue of the rock.

I feel fresh amazement in the where of things; I see that the tumble of comic faces
among the sticks and curled willow leaves

is only a facade to gentle me into open acquiescence for a new journey
I have already begun.

Prematurely, perhaps,
I wedge myself in.

Contents

Judicare vivos et mortuos 7

Acknowledgments 11

1 *Why not opening fanfare?*

Original Flamboyance 14
Worried About Birds 16
The Sense in Which Things Are Alive 18
I Need to Know This 19
Going to St. Ives 20
The Sky We Could Always Count On in Our Grief 22
Migration 24
So Gratefully Then My Eyes 25
Meaning Well: A Fable 26
Sunning 27
Willow Close 28

2 *This may be how I discovered certain things are impossible.*

Until You Can Draw the Horse 32
A Piano's Perspective 34
Snowy Egret: The Birth of Motion 36
Lightening 38
Non-Compliance 39
The Waterfall Is a Volcano 40
Glimpses of the Garden Rat from the Kitchen Window 42
Keep 44
The Basic Photo 45
Transcending on Demand 46

3 *What if everyone had to choose once and for all?*

Gavotte 50
The Day Arrives 52
Veteran 53
Coffee House Consort 54
But I Was Not Expecting 55
Let There Be 56
Landscape of a Sparrow 58

The Natural World	59
Bear Dream	60
Canyon Protocol	62

4 *Only the hand of god, broken at the fingers, holds me.*

No Title Yet	66
My Son Remembers the Sun	68
A Small Dark Bird	70
Before and After	72
Preposition	74
The Enunciation	76
Eavesdropping	77
A Catalogue of Silences	78
My Mother's Elbows	79
Holding Off	80

5 *Deftly invisible, the voice.*

Love a Geometry	84
The Psychoanalysis of House-Love	86
Auntie Dwendy and the Toast Butterer's Apprentice	88
Occiput	90
An Instance of the Feather	91
Canyon Wren	92
Hinge	94
The Piano Dreamed	95
Another Reason	96
The Robin's Temporary	97

About the Author	99

Acknowledgments

The author extends gratitude to the editors of the following publications in which these poems first appeared:

Catamaran: "Worried About Birds," Spring 2020

Nimrod International Journal: "Preposition," Spring 2020

Plum Tree Tavern: "Beak, " November 2017, https://theplumtreetavern.blogspot.com

Seventh Quarry: "Hinge" and "Lightening," 2020

America, We Call Your Name (anthology): "Another Reason," Sixteen Rivers Press, 2018

And If the Dead Do Dream (chapbook): "My Son Remembers the Sun," Uttered Chaos Press, Eugene, Oregon, 2016

1

Why not opening fanfare?

Original Flamboyance

A million years ago humans
gained "control of fire"
which meant cooking but also spiffing up
              our rituals.

Fire covered
the gaps
in the plots.
          Since then

     we've relished
           (wildly risky)
the burning part of any story the part
we must outrun again again again.

Hell forbids uncertainty, but
             the essential fickleness of fire
             assures degrees of misery
even on a small scale
between bad, worse and worst.

I once counted out my brother's days
in phone calls & daffodil petals:
the petals falling in my garden,
his life a continent away.

We are meant to believe
in a forever-ish universe, adept at joy, where
     every tiny house-ant struggles
to avoid the dust pan, the sponge, the poison,

and each tree screams
under the flames,
as if love of life is primary too
in other philosophies.

So, why does the one who giggles
have to be compost in the end? Which of us

is finally going to stand up like David
before Goliath and ask:
      "Is this indeed the best of all possible universes
      as we have been told?—and if not—

      here is what we need to do. . . .

Worried About Birds

I am worried about the birds again.
As I walk past the library, I stop to tie my shoe
so the young man in front of me, loudly conducting
clouds with his cigarette, will not feel me at his back,
will not veer again into the street.

> *Dutilleux!* comes into my head, and I whisper it: "Dutilleux!"
> The name sounds exactly how a winter wren in February
> quietly practices the opening of her song.

Did I always worry about the birds, I mean, before?
This is different from cats and windmills and people with guns.

This is about what they eat. I mean,
when they peck on the open ground. Has anyone done studies
about whether juncos swallow, for example, cigarette butts?
And if so—? And if not
what are they taking from the surface of the earth that's
   keeping them alive?

> *Rapscallion!* comes into my head, and I whisper it:
>   "Rapscallion!"
> I pick at the skin on my thumbs, rub my hand behind my
> neck, scratch the small scabs on my shoulders.

If nobody smoked, would be good; if nobody had a reason to
   start smoking,
would be even better. Smoking begins as a displacement activity,
but then it starts keeping you sane.

You need a displacement for the displacement.
You need to start worrying about birds.

Which is not totally obsessive. It's more like rolling your head around
in a slow and complicated way as if it were a kaleidoscope.

Even if you can't see inside, you can hear
all the little pieces ganging up, tipping into new patterns; you want
to wait for the best one, then stop.

> *Come de light an' I wanna go home.*

The Sense in Which Things Are Alive

A spoon, quiet in the drawer,
when set down carelessly on the kitchen counter
will jiggle in a fixed pattern of diminishing arcs

like a piano string humming its way back
to an achievable stillness.

Not the way, landing on a twig,
a small bird knits up the corner of your eye
        like a snowflake—
                and if you turn to look at it head-on

will have disappeared
through the wide swinging doors
of what it means to be among the living.
                The spoon

is a heartier sort, so that the morning breakfast ritual
                        inevitably includes
a constant shushing on my part, a light
laying on of hands when a utensil will not quieten
without its pivot-dance. I am surrounded always

by the nascent but unruly vigor
of spoons (forks knives) holding, in proportion,
the same geometric capacities
as a Stonehenge
       or a gothic cathedral.

I Need to Know This

When birds begin to murmur from those pastel, blotted distances
at the first turning of a summer afternoon —
                signaling the not-yet-but-soon

arrival of a different light—you take this as the future

blowing its inaudible horn. Children hear it, and they
        answer with the mumble language of contentment
              that makes its own words.

But here in the forest, your eyes insist
        the light has not changed, twilight
            is hours away, much less dark.

Might these sounds also hold different meanings?

            Why not opening fanfare—or the constant chanting
            of the wheel of turquoise
            that a ship's engine spools up
                      from the bottom of the sea?

Going to St. Ives

Only a mother could have given such a permission:
                first to notice, then to enjoy
the tiny shift the voice makes
between talking to a carrot and talking to a turnip
when one is chopping vegetables on a winter afternoon.

I once knew this, and so much more. That the dead,
going back maybe 5000 years,
all that time
have been stockpiling the light-dust of their bodies for igneous rock.

In pencil I wrote "speak" at the top of the page
then immediately erased it. I wanted to write
"Speak poetry as the only language from now on,"
but I didn't know how to say that in poetry yet.

Like the riddle about St. Ives, where everything seems to hinge
upon the meaning of the verb "met."
                                But maybe

      everything does depend on
"How Many Are Going To St. Ives."
If we really need to know, we must investigate
all possibilities for meeting.

        Otherwise
      the incarnation of each new species
      would have been merely an act of postponement.

At the dining table, my brother would challenge me
while we were eating dessert: "What am I thinking about
    at this very minute? You have three guesses!"

If I had said "Chocolate ice cream is yummy!"
     this, at least, would have to be right.
But I fell for the circus and picnic and seashore options
every time.

_____

*   As I was going to St. Ives.
     I met a man with seven wives
     Every wife had seven sacks
     Every sack had seven cats
     Every cat had seven kits
     Kits, cats, sacks, wives
     How many were going to St. Ives?

The Sky We Could Always Count On in Our Grief

Let the suffering begin!
The universal early morning cry
hangs in the air above the railroad tracks where the women go
to relieve themselves before the men are awake.

Walk 7 miles to work
split, tear, cut, crush, shatter, flatten.
Walk 7 miles home. Eat, sleep,
make another child.

Look up! Look up! Where is the sun?
Still a bull up there but
gagged into silence by the ash.

Everything is enormous, irregular beyond healing.
The Great Necromancer Sky we could always count on
      in our grief
has retreated into his house of sticks.
Alive is not the same as Not-Dead.

Ash drifts down, white in air,
gray on surfaces—smears
under the fingers, ash snivels and smothers,
inveigles-into, chokes, pretends
fire has gone away, the soldiers will not return for you.

Lies, lies, lies. Your legs are numb, your stomach a post,
Dead is not the same as not-Alive.

Everything is enormous, irregular beyond healing
You walk between stacks of trees that once were lions,

cough through their exuded dusks;
you crawl upon towering immensities of discarded bark
like an insect, filling the holes left by the crew before you:
Fill, mold, flatten,
scrape, heat and bend, sand, swage and polish.

You realize you will never be allowed to stop until you, too,
lose your limbs. The sky has closed; you must whisper a code to
   the trees
to let you through.

Migration

A hyphen of sound   tugs
  the rim of your ear

"They're coming!"
  you say, you say   "Wait!"

You summon your several selves
from the dreaming fields

Quick! Before the pointed key
you call for

disguise
as preemptive nonchalance

escape
into a noise of your own choosing

But your eager ear mistakes
the need and

the flock's upon you
Merging at the entrance

the V tumbles in, you
follow   follow   follow

So Gratefully Then My Eyes

Driving home in the dark I said
to my steering wheel:
"I still believe something else about the instant!"
Not the moment—the instant.

Those summer afternoons when light collapses
as if it had a stroke, and goes off to hospital
leaving us to not-notice on its behalf.

But still glows from sought-for faces
going by, going by
                as we deal with
all this looking-without-seeing we must get done
before our time is up.

So gratefully then, my eyes can disengage, can revert to
       only gazing, watching, reflecting like a mirror.

               I watch a red squirrel's tail
leave off its connection to the animal
and float out
from under the garden trellis
as a plume of fire.

The rest of the squirrel lopes
around the flower beds
with a walnut in its mouth.

We both come home
with a new set of bones between our shoulder blades,
warm from the transfer.

Meaning Well: A Fable

We were hungry among the stones and brown decaying leaves.
But they were handing out souls from the parked trucks not food—
souls in net bags
for us to carry, to inhale their clouds
of virtues, soft and shining.

> *some things are so beautiful you can't eat them*

How do you feel? they asked, and we answered:
Like a silver leaf and someone very small riding the edge of it,
down to water.

> *sometimes you are so hungry you will eat the beautiful things*
> *even if you know their names*

How do you feel? they asked again, and sliding our silky new souls
between our fingers, we answered:
Like the light coming off the living ferns has climbed into our mouths
and up into the bones around our eyes.

> *sometimes you forget the names of anything you cannot eat*

Our outlines grow more distant
as our hollow insides slowly fill with yellow clay.
We can no longer fly because
we ate our wings. Apparently, the souls were meant
as parachutes, but we are here already, without having
fallen.

Sunning

In the sun on a log
we sit. I forget why we came.
The edges of the world go round our ears
like the wall of a snow fort
as it's being built,
      shiny, patted-down
          mittenfull by mittenfull. No roof.
River swinging under our feet.

I could ask "Did you ever even *think*
about putting a roof on a snow fort?"
but there is no need.
River swinging under our feet.

Feeling the sun cap my head
I know it as is has come to be,
molten, seeping into our nightmares
      yet also, as it once was.

To give   *that*
                to you.

We now, still sharing it
as slices of chilled melon passed
in secret from tongue to tongue.

Willow Close

How close can a human
come to a willow?

All its legends whisper of water
touched and entered.
The under-earth clacks and shuttles
with siphoning businesses, water
shinnies upward behind the
bark.

I sit erect on the marble bench
body open to willow descending
in a blading of small suns.

Might I slake
the curling branches beside my cheek
with the slow hemorrhage
from the centers of my feet?

2

*This may be how I discovered
certain things are impossible.*

Until You Can Draw the Horse

In sixth grade I drew horses with Linda.
She lay on the floor of her room
(I sat on a chair)
sketching the long muzzles
the perfect arches of the necks.

This may be how I discovered
certain things are impossible.

> *the line of careless scorn between eye and nostril*

I began riding lessons at the same stable
where Linda went
but not at the same time.
I fell off a horse.

> *the rampant sinews making willing eclipses of themselves*

She drew daily with her right hand
and mean spirits; horses poured from her.

I took up the violin.
I practiced an hour a day.

To play a scale correctly
is to hear each note
a split second before your finger touches
the neck of the instrument.
This is impossible.

The ways of drawing wrong the curves of a horse's body
are virtually infinite.

the wide forehead not tending towards
any geometric form,
a raft across the top of the face
the eye a dark star, a portal.

On the walls of Chauvet Cave
the necks are perfect;
the artists worked quickly, did not erase.

A Piano's Perspective

In the bottom right corner of today's real-life painting
the perspective is wrong. A black object
the size of a beetle, but shaped

like a grand piano, suddenly explodes,
filling the corner with an inky fog.

I try to brush it off as merely
        a mote in the eye that
        compares to everything else
        as a pea to a mattress.

But I know it's a piano.
Not a camel, but a piano
entering and re-entering the eye's needle
in some desperate attempt to get my attention.

I squint down upon the asymmetrical blot
lodged in my peripheral vision
silent, but nonetheless sending out in waves
a call that only someone guilty
through a very specific chain of events could
recognize as hopeless to evade.
        Why did you run off and leave me so long ago?
        All these years I could have helped you out.
        I was your panther soul. . . .

Looming, as it rolls
        purposefully in my direction
this piano (doubtless my 1923 Steinway O with its crazed finish)
is becoming, as the dust settles,
like a teenage gypsy telling her first fortune.

I feel it creak with suppressed secrets
from the musical part of my past,
the part not only does nobody else know, but nobody else
can know.

I am helpless now, snagged by a single *What-if?* By several sets
of familiar echoes.

A sort of heaving, charcoal sadness envelops me.

The piano snickers as it presents its clearly outlined
unfragmented self to my prewounded soul. It has only pretended
to explode, and as it comes closer I hear it lecturing me
from our last conversation three decades ago:
> *You realize—People in the 16th century*
> *listening to Orlando de Lassus*
> *would have felt a **strangeness**, just like we do.*
> *Certain music is never normal, even in its own time;*
> *it practices without us.*

How could a piano possibly have known that, you may ask,
   it wasn't invented yet?
Ha! I say. And Ha!

Snowy Egret: The Birth of Motion

The shape
     of a body
the body of a bird
a long white bird
     that walks
     its one-limbed self

        across the water
by splitting in two

by opening and closing
over and under
     the pond's rim.
                The body
        splits
            and reunites
        opens into a jaw
           closes
into a slim
     ophidian
        stick

so that the bird moves forward
     by cleaving, uncleaving.

When the upper bird dips
its neck to touch
        the surface   to close
     the circle
        again
the reflection rises
at the other end, offering
to become the bottom lip
     of a mouth

                                                    but fails
    to rise
      into a full line   or cannot —

leaving capacity   always
    for leaving.

Lightening

The blue Camas flowers in the meadow
      have stopped time.
I cover my ears.

All around, the newly-leafing trees
are empty of crows, who—unserrated and somewhat oval silhouettes—
have offered themselves through winter dusks

as temporary leaves, a signal generosity.
I tilt my head back and see one up there
caught in a crossfire of beams, *outlined*.

Engaged in a shadow play
with the branch beneath him, his body spits
silver-gold sparks. Deftly
he flouts certain properties
of the table of elements.

God was afraid in the Garden of Eden
that good and evil would leap into the same
balance pan, and prove a different point.

He paced, terrible in visage, hiding
until they plucked and ate.

This crow kindles a lichened branch,
      sups on an earlier version of the story;
more strips of sky drop
to the grass under our feet.

Non-Compliance
—Winter Solstice 2020

Sun caught
prowling along the ground
behind an old board fence.

Sun addled
glides forward
(not up), plows a level
horizon, sucking
glow out of
the weaker shadows.

Riding the freight cars,
all afternoon, Sun fails
to arc above
the tracks.
Sun crouches
on its invisible skateboard
growling low in its
furnace throat:

Winter Solstice? I'll never make it
See the great pieces ripped out of me
already old flesh flung loose
onto the cinnabar hills
I'll hunker down,
hide among the gravestones,
light a cigarette.

Reduced to a gormless cinder sun
teeters on the birdbath's
rim.

The Waterfall Is a Volcano
   —Watson Falls, Umpqua River, Oregon

At the beginning, water
        and water plunging
           to stone and stone still
                half molten.

Mist from the pool
        gathers
around the eyes, unfurrowing
into smoke, to steam, to ashes.

Rare gusts of wind
push the veil sideways.

When she looked down at us,
my grandmother's eyes were filled
with bruised blossoms.
        The petals

brushed past her temples,
her cheeks
        as if she were fleeing her childhood winds,
        though they did not pursue.

My grandmother harridan/diva
whose name was Rose.

Once her husband fell
down the hall stairs, crumpling
like a butterfly
        by the grandfather clock.

Leaning back
at the bottom of this waterfall,

I see white
blossom down in furrows tightly furled
      and strike the pool rising.

We grandchildren basked
in the concrete fish pond like vertical fish
      forbidden with our faces
      to touch water. All summer we inhaled
wet sunlight
blew it out like smoke.
He fell through clear air
figment by figment.

We blamed the cigarettes.

Glimpses of the Garden Rat
from the Kitchen Window

Listen with your elbows, I tell myself, unable to hear
even the scuffing of his small feet.

As one black, glossy, bright-eyed rat
disappears into the downed thicket of bamboo branches,
its many bowers. . . .

> O rounded heart-closet embrace!
> I know that low green tunnel, the hunched crawl, the arrival
>   at the level dirt place in the center. Own secret.

❇

Here's where the curve goes still: glue dries
on the piano's steam-spliced rim, the molten metal hardens in
    its mold,
            river meander breaks off into a slough —

pliers, flame, sledge-hammer, clamps,
kill the gesture but not
by straightening it out.

❇

The curb that lines the straight street is arrested tendency,
a tail caught in an outward flick.

Each line retains the potential of its other shape.
Even a small dip in the pavement
may pull the bicyclist down.

The rat moves along the fence
his arched back poised
for a leap or a fold.

Keep

> *... the dream-generated geography of the body*
> —Oscar Miro Quesada

If the squirrel starts to cross
                and the car keeps coming.

If the squirrel pauses
                and the car keeps coming.

If the car veers and the squirrel
also.

Into my rear view mirror I have cried "No! No!"
                                            for them
removing both hands
from the steering wheel.

There is space behind the heart
        to carve out a little room
                like a cave behind a waterfall.

On a low shelf, my mother's love of violets,
her fear of the dark.

She told me once, "I have this dream
        of a lion hiding in the closet,"
but I think she meant a lioness.

If the sun went out
for the length of time it takes a human to die
for lack of breathing.

The day my mother slapped me in the face
and we stood leaning together like two clocks
with their counterweights cut.

She must have taken my hand.

The Basic Photo

    —Evdilos, Ikaria, Greece, October 2012

Looking down a long white stairway
                          ill-lit, back-street night
on the bottom stair
        the lost one is not like the others
a black cat   elongates
to pass beneath
the marble arch

        (but what actually happens)
the front half slides out of view
the back half
        (stays longer)
disappears in another place.

I pull my sweater around my elbows
and lean further into the dark.

Three steps above me
my son in the cloud
burgles the internet connection
through the walls of the hotel
closed now for the season.

Above us a rind of moon
    (goes wane wane)
Will we   remember?

My cells have eaten it.

Transcending on Demand

On Patmos every evening we would take the goat path
uphill through the stones
               the way goats climb
the most impossible cliffs—*levitating*
from boulder to boulder, ignoring
what's between.

And we would enter Chora,
the village on top, to seek
the single restaurant in the center.

The streets
were a labyrinth impossible to map,
yet each time they led us to this place.

The whitewashed building, a few tables in front
precarious on the flagstones.
The same couple drinking ouzo; the same guys
huddled over their games of tavli. We went in

from the dark porch, the bright passage through
the kitchen to the cloistered terrace
above the distant sea, of which
we had heard continuous rumor.

Each slow dinner ends; returning tomorrow,
      the only option,
will involve goats and a steeply winding path.
But while we sit, speaking in three languages over wine,
if someone mentions transcending we would likely say
we'd rather something came down here instead.

Blue and yellow, perhaps, like a lion strolling along a seashore.

3

*What if everyone had to choose
once and for all?*

Gavotte

The dilemma presents itself
through a song in my head—the gavotte
from Bach's Sixth English Suite –
while I am hiking a forest path:

> *What if everyone had to choose*
> *once and for all*
> *whether to live indoors or outdoors?*

The choice is
shade and the possibility of wolves
or crossing barefoot a quarry
of seared gray stones.

They say the path over the sharp rocks is
      hot, slow.

              While I decide
I walk on a ridge covered with tears
no, I mean trees. I am looking for footholds
in the great cliff across from me. What
did we do last time? But you are not here.

Leaves rustle against my shoes, my
heels thump downbeats,
or are they upbeats?
Should it be four-and-four, or
five-and-one, then two? Bach comes in
in so many ways,
    through the nose, the chest, the pelvis.

      I face the cliff
now like a sunflower, steadfast
at the end of her day. Am I so drawn
by the possibility of heat and stone?—No,
the other thing.

My eyes go yellow and green,
brown and green, yellow and brown,
my silly dappled eyes say
"Outside! Outside!"
There would be porches
for common ground between us.

The Day Arrives

Yesterday, that meadow along the highway
was safely horizontal —
a short, fat meadow gleaming greenly
behind a managed forest of anorexic alders,
meadow with a belly on it, jolly
but docile.

Today that meadow seems preoccupied;
it rises, almost vertical behind the trees,
flapping lightly, exposing stretch marks, stains,
crushed-nap smudges. Rabidly
it sops up the morning's yellow luminosity
like a toast set loose among the eggs.

The anemic, gracile alders
are beginning to bend,
almost to squint, or turn their trunks around
like owls
in a collective quake of anticipation.
What day is this?

Their roots have been bound for so long,
assuming they remember
the terms of the original agreement,
they may still stumble as they're walking out.

Veteran

When it was over he returned to the sea
his veins caked with unholy compliances

the world now shrunken into an equivocal
cloak of murmurings, transparent but not
invisible—textured to induce
a cloudbank on the tongue

and blurred vision, a most welcome foil
to the framed clarity of the heartless.
A shriek and pound of engines had long filled his
water-loving space; now these
waves again, or at least

he felt a different word stirring at the base
of his jaw, in the hollow
behind the earlobe.

He walked on the damp sand as "he"

without bleeding anywhere inside or out,
his breathing quieted, but not his voice
which now he could set loose
from his throat unshaped. He reeled,

remembered

one moment when he was twelve and knew his entire body
as only a face—oval dumb plate of a thing, floating –

> in the way of geese who fly high over buildings
> looking, looking, but they cannot
> at those moments (nor do they need to) see.

Coffee House Consort

   —for Joan Benson

Across the table sipping hot cider
this woman was once
the finest clavichordist in the world.

At that time star clusters were forming
in a blue crush of molecules. It was the year
of the monkey, or maybe the snake.

"Nobody remembers me now." She speaks
precisely, as if giving advice.
"Expressiveness is out of fashion."

The man carrying his coffee past our table
says "Look! Everyone's wearing pink today!"
We take a furtive peek, and it is true!

I look at her hands, expecting them
to make everything clear
about the great shift in expressiveness.

Her technique, she tells me,
required lifting each finger
without any of the others moving.

Slightly curved over the table, her back.
Holding her glass in that same arc,
her preternatural hands.

"I wouldn't play C.P.E.—any of it
the same way now," she says,
demolishing her earlier argument.

But I Was Not Expecting

                  For weeks now
an elephant appears in my garden
every morning, browsing briefly and with
                                     great delicacy
        among the parsley and kale.
The bad dreams about the ocean have left me at last.
The river has changed back into
                        a snake.
                                  Cautiously optimistic,
     I begin to believe these events signal the onset
     of the journeyman stage
                             of my training.

Let There Be

I hear my mother talking in the kitchen.
"It's dishy-washy time!" she says,
my mother talking in my kitchen
in another person's voice,
in a high and cheerful voice.

Not speaking her own words,
my mother, never spoke this way
making a falseness in her voice
to fool another person to come and beg
admission to this small circle, into
this special space

before the sink, as if the cleaning
of the dishes comes before
the eating, as if she had been waiting
all day for entertainment
at the sink, her hands from previous soapy
water dried and cracking, her hands
from the dirty soapy waters.

My mother's voice says altered words to fool
another person that she might be willing
to offer up her special place.

It is myself I'm hearing in the kitchen,
my pretend voice is filling the air, is
stirring the air before the sink,
I am the one standing
here alone, clearing a conjured
space, a happy holy dancing floor—
making an after dinner shiny time

when all the dishes lower themselves
obediently into clean soapy water, move
under the brush, when all the dishes
rise again from dirty soapy water,
levitate unto the bright gush of clear water
coming from the faucet, hot water
hurtful to hands. Soon they will sail
winking and sparkling into the drying rack,
making light in the kitchen where I
have turned my back upon the sink to dance.

Landscape of a Sparrow

Comes into view on a high twig
a sparrow's soft underbelly
with its meadows and hedgerows,
creek beds and thorns.

And though I cannot call out *which sparrow*
      from this side of the bird,
I know a map when I see one.

I am reminded that every day
Earth's invisible shadow-body
flows along ancient pathways
      beneath our feet
in response to the shift in solar winds.

Already, someone has begun today's story,
exhaling it like the hiss of possibilities
      when you pry up an old barbed wire fence
embedded in a hillside of vines.

And though I cannot call out which sparrow
I can suggest a new word for *lion rampant*
upon this tender, feathered tapestry.

The Natural World

Autumn colors jiggle on the bushes and vines
outside the chain link fence that surrounds

the wrecking yard. Nature, ever plotting another leap
into the inner weeds, volunteers as a spy

inside the brand new warehouse-of-old-parts
her dragon familiar idling among the geriatric

computer cables, printers, mounds of twisted
metal guts formerly humming and austere.

Meanwhile, out here dark figures with clipboards
climb in and out of low vehicles

but nobody comes to sell me the office chair.
Soundless in the drizzle, stripped and staved-in cars

already picked-over by the wrecking trucks,
still hunker in the muddy grass,

disguising themselves as raw materials again.
Like running out of a cathedral to get out of the rain.

Engine idling, car and body intact,
I need to keep moving, the year's closing down.

Across the highway the abandoned solar panel factory
that blocks my view of distant, gentle, limpid

beautiful purpling hills
might already be "the view."

Bear Dream

There are no adverbs in my dream of bears.
The animals might appear
       anywhere
among the trees, they
move like blots,
I cannot see their eyes, I don't know
              I don't know.

At any one moment I
glance over to see if they (always more than one) have gone or
            never arrived. My dream
has nothing to do with them.

I am walking along a valley floor
lit by a leaky pinkish sky.
I am walking to meet someone ahead
who has turned back to wait there.
On my left along the hill that is the bears,'

an open forest of lovely dark and thick-boled trees,
from any of which—a shape may detach
      to cross
indifferently, the muffling ground.
        How—if one happens upon or
        appears in the vicinity of
                my only partly
                eaten but still largely
                fresh and delighted heart?

Terror can be postponed, but not destroyed.
I always lift my eyes.
This is not a nightmare, the bears are mostly potential here.

If the stars sped up, would they too give that impression
of coming out of somewhere other than a place?

This is richness, now the bears are wearing masks
I stare, expecting to see their eyes
glowing like lilies through the slits. I slow down,
    their heads dip, bodies
        rise. Something about a dance.
Here my dream retracts; to slide me out again.
If I could only explain. . . .

Canyon Protocol

    —Canyon de Chelly, Arizona

The not-saying of a boulder
differs from
the not-saying of an entire cliff.

Their facing-out is similar
but not the same.

Disregard huge and silent.
The inertia of twist
(could be a factor).

The possibility-quotient for a
canyon wall depends upon
whatever optimum flexing
it can still carry through
with.

Surface scourings
are orchestrated by water, sun, wind.

Deep certainties clash
here at canyon's edge,
fluted and fretted by pine
juniper, swallow, raven,
lizard, rabbit, cougar,
mesquite, blue lichen
and a myriad of grasses

into a rhythm, even almost
a set of chords. As we lie
on the rim rocks in the shade

we are nourished by
the canyon's old gestures
spare
in their own realm,
hugely generous in ours.

4

*Only the hand of god, broken
at the fingers, holds me.*

No Title Yet

I—The Riff

My dearest wish would be for all humans to die together at the same age—all gazillion of us, who have loved deeply and well through our allotted lifetimes—having made enough of a holy ruckus in our chains that we finally earned the capacity
                              to end, or continue,
                                          together.

II—First Consequence

I am holding the bent finger of god.
I am holding the cracked and broken hand
of the god of here and now,
the broken, cracked,
with rough edges like a plant pot
                              shattered—
but not the shards only, the
hand still attached to the
wrist, the arm, the elbow.
The wounded. The wound.
Resting inside my half
open palm but not
filling it snugly because
my hands are (were) yet whole,
only the hand of the god, broken
at the fingers, holds
me.

III—Were Falling

Eyes were falling from the trees
on a cloudy winter afternoon
as I in a maroon Chrysler
drove slowly into a narrow paved
street in the Boston suburbs; its sign
at the bottom read "Prospect Hill Road."

Eyes were filling these now leafless fruit trees
that lined the street like a small orchard
interrupted in the middle by a narrow
drive that went straight up,
up to a distant top of a hill

where it stopped or turned
out of sight. The eyes were whispering
as they slowly drifted down
from the trees,
not as though
they had been placed there, or belonged either.

Small and identical, shiny, transparent
like the replacement eyes for a
set of stuffed rabbits or bears.
Shiny brown irises against a soft white
background, the eyes
did not seem to be visible but only
a kind of swarm quietly resting
on the twigs for awhile—a flock of them
on their way through the memory circuits
of the woman in the auto parked
at the bottom of the hill.
Where I began many things for the first time
so very long ago.

My Son Remembers the Sun

So often when I speak about the sun, an enormous red rose entangles itself in my tongue. But I do not have the capacity to remain silent.
       —Odysseus Elytis

So, in the redwood grove when we talked about dying
you said "I would really miss my mind" and
I knew exactly what you meant. I nodded "Yeah,
assembling your own mind through a lifetime
is like creating a new person from scratch."
You grinned, "Dying seems so wasteful after all that work."

You and I had talked about this. How a single day should be enough.
Or for those two yellow butterflies
chasing each other round and round a distant fir,
maybe every orbit equals one year.

"Details—" you continued, "it's all in the details, and God
is a big-picture guy. Up there—." You pointed, and stopped.
We were under a tree so tall the sun hung just above
the tip, slowly unfolding its tarp of hourly motes, spilling them
onto our knees. We had abandoned the hike to sit
on a slope so steep our chins were tilted 45 degrees.
There came into my head then, all at once, a way to explain
the essential difference between right-and-left, and east-and-west.
This is what I need to say to him—your brother, not you.
I took a breath to speak.

But you stood up, covered in almost-horizontal light
leaning your head back, facing the fractured sky "If there were
a god, wouldn't it *have to be* the sun?" I turned slightly,
to face the nearest tree. I had just touched its airy outer bark
and knew I was miles from the central core. *Which might be fire.
Or not.*
Which I must now spend another lifetime trying to reach.

"*That's* why we need so many minds!" I said softly,
"so we can go slowly enough, handing off in relays,"
 but you stayed silent, nailed
 by a single beam, before I could add
"You and I have talked about this," though we hadn't yet.

A Small Dark Bird

Had not been thinking of her at all
feeling a little dizzy
sitting in the dark gazing at nothing
weary at the end of the day,
     I whispered my mother's name.

Hers and mine both start with the same letter,
are both somewhat rare.
     How does it sound? I've almost forgot
         a word I hardly ever spoke before –
So I tried it in the air.

And I heard my voice as someone else

while I sat in the dark on her behalf,
someone else
     whispering her name.

Inside, a quiet
opened
like a narrow lagoon lined with reeds, a quiet
memory
her own, not mine.

         I did not know it,
only felt it pass through me on its way out.
I opened my mouth,
     whispered again
with breath enough so her name need not touch my throat.

And it flew
like a small dark bird.

My mother, being called to by someone she loved
an instant in her actual life, the memory caught for years.

Maybe her younger sister—my aunt—calling softly
from the front porch, through the screen door at dusk,
she inside next to one of her father's clocks —
     Wake up, Aggie, wake up
     I have something to tell you!
caught in a cobweb on the ceiling.

       I whispered as a sort of test,
hers and mine both start with the same letter, are both
   somewhat rare.

I tried it in the air, and felt it firm
            like a small chocolate, the last one in the box,
unseen in its crinkled black and shiny paper boat
          now rushing out through the locks.

Before and After

Once an enormous god with an enormous hand
at the end of his long skinny arm—
        reached into the
      (way-before-anything-else)
                              cosmic mist
        and pulled out
a squalling puppy by the scruff of its neck.

    This is not a fact.

Every August I lie on my back on a dark hill
looking into the night sky. Sometimes I see

a meteor that was not there suddenly
not there again.

This must be how the world began—
as an echo orphaned
      from its source.

Today a cabbage butterfly flew arrow-straight across
my kitchen window, heading east, its path
made a golden-section
between the top and bottom of the frame.

From across the room, remembering this, I wonder
                      again
why the sky does not more often perform
these spontaneous cohesions—
                why are we not

regularly struck by objects falling from overhead
as the yet-unformed serve out their (almost) infinite sentences
of improbability? How often swaths of fine mist
      must scrape against prickly wodges
of atoms gone all widdershins

      and precipitate as something prior
      to a meteor—

a clear bell sound in the air just below the ceiling
of a busy restaurant during Sunday brunch—a puppy,

or a white butterfly's small galumph
           as quarter moon, waxing into sunrise.

Preposition

It's morning so I must drive back to the hospital on my own.
I know we crossed the river in the dark.
The bridge was on 12th, the hotel's on 5th. Piece of cake.

A block out of the parking garage I arrive
at the corner of 4th Street and 4th Avenue.

Doing the logic, I turn the wrong way
into a one-way street. Backtrack to 3rd Avenue,
hunker down beside a curb to breathe.

Then the prepositions arrive,
each one a little metal chute,
each one depositing me outside
a different door
         door of indigo
         door of Styrofoam
         door of fish whiskers no longer attached

               door belonging to the Queen of Spades.

Growing smaller and later behind my steering wheel,
unable to pray, I think about the divine.

If everything is divine—or at least alive—what about the non-things?
    [Like prepositions]? And questions:
        How long has it been since I was a cat?
        Is "since" a preposition?

A preposition may be more like the Higgs boson than
   the Queen of Spades.

    And don't capitalize boson for cripe sake,
        or you may be DOOMED.
    Nor insert a hyphen between the two words,
        lest they get the wrong idea
            about their relationship.
    Nor place an apostrophe after Higgs to indicate possession.

Here's the thing: the Higgs boson has no primary purpose,
there is only secondary purpose. Only. I just now figured that out.

Unlike the divine. Maybe like the preposition, although I doubt it.
Exactly like this grid of unrelated streets with similar names.
They would have called
me if he were dying.

Remember, the contract goes like this: *You will have a short*
   awakening, but it will be glorious.
Or maybe it was "frumious?"? He will get a kick out of that.
It seems impossible to sit with secondary purpose for long.
I will go one more block, turn around
and head for 12th Street. Or was it 12th Avenue?
The river must be nearby.

The Enunciation

I fell
in love with the way he pronounced
"muddy."

I heard him say it once
softly
from across a busy room.

I fell
with the cathedral on my back
I carry for the bells and the equivalent of bells

as sanctuary to those holy instruments
who must propel their unruly musicks
by shredding each pure tone
into metallic shards of noise—

who have risked so much
on our behalf
in the belfry's armory
among the half-eaten rats,
the long-deafened pigeons.

Certain low words may be preserved
inside the rare silences that only here occur—
a long distillation of extinct owls'
calls have pooled in crevices of stone
behind the cliff face—and ring out

whenever an eclipse peels
off the sun's body again.
I did not see him

and my knees did buckle under the weight
of his enunciation.

Eavesdropping

I cross a footbridge I have already crossed
over a small brown creek
look down

not at its color
or set of flickering shapes
       but a gesture made by *the whole creek*.

As if I had eavesdropped
and been caught.

The way, in the silence of January snow,
trees may send out the noise
of a horse blowing after taking a drink.

Or when I wake at night to hear you
beside me listening to your heart
doing something
          distinctly geologic,
    to remind you
how it will be as stone.

The brown bubbling stream seems to be
      slowing its arrival at the bridge
by way of a complicated curve.
                Futile perhaps, but

rarely does a stream so deliberately
—as if by baring its neck—
        invite
the searing kiss.

A Catalogue of Silences

World, I am saturate
with your holy dusks.
They still come
more often
than I had imagined,
        so that

even midway through this siege of plague and fires
all that can bob and dangle
    [the pots & pans hanging
    on the kitchen beam softly
    following their
        diminishing arcs into
            pewter whispers]

may do so in the fullness of an earned quiet.

We may have been taught
that everything is always moving—
but actually
only almost everything is (always moving) so that
what is not (moving) can regularly
disappear—as if it had never been.

Only if we could hold in regard
each molecule and mote of sunlight
as a photograph about to be
    snapped
would those items truly motionless
flare up briefly as the unassailable universe

we've been hoping to find intact.

My Mother's Elbows

Sometimes standing among a small group of people
all relaxed, with our hands by our sides,
I remember again how I loved my mother's elbows.

Viewed from behind the angle from the shoulders a
slight backward arc, was perfect as was
the awkward slenderness suggesting—particulars to me,
not in themselves you understand—but it seems

I had always wished to recognize the girl in her,
whom I could not know directly
any other way.

Forgetting for years at a time
only to be reminded at the end of
a tai chi class today when eleven students

in our seventies stood in a circle
around our elderly teacher
as firmly and tenderly as if we were lions

protecting our cubs, remembering again
that we were growing something among
the skin and bones of us—inevitable risk

in a mutual but deeply buried love.

Holding Off

> *Your disappearing holds off for awhile.*
> —Patricia Fargnoli

And if not for the reddish glint from a single strand of my hair
resting on top of the computer keyboard—close close

to the path of no return—if not

for its gleam carelessly unfurled
between zero at the top, V at the bottom, not
yet having floated down

an hour ago when the whole room was still dark,
now here among all the vanished others

sealing up forever this last journey from
useful to irrelevant in a thread-like curl
scarcely able to muster the requirements for a shadow
much less bear the weight of one.

But auburn instead of white, signifying less recent,
closer to the bone, the inner reserves, last to let go.

This one is still mine. I see as from the eyes of my two sons
who are sitting awhile in my study after my recent death.
Together they endure passage
through the gamut of remnants still arriving
and leaving, caught in the normal shift

of in and out and in again. Here among boxes and files,
where no trace of my bedroom slippers remains
in the recently vacuumed rug. They sit on the floor, their
bodies bent forward, each resting his head on his closed hand,
eyes closed waiting for the soft shushing of their mother's life
to finish—please finish!—its smooth transition
into a wholly different kind of necessary usefulness—and
taking this in
        one breath
                at a time.

5

Deftly invisible, the voice

Love a Geometry

Statistically he was redundant: an 86-year-old man with
 congestive heart failure,
macular degeneration, and a growing tendency to fall down
for no apparent reason.

In our early days, my obsession was how the Asian Fairy-Bluebird
related to the piano, that the color of its wings occurs gratuitously,
a side effect of angle, not a result of pigment saturation.
—Therefore, (I pointed out to him) geometry can trigger motion
simply by position, and redundancy
can be a poised thing, a rattlesnake-in-the-brake.

Inside the 1722 piano replica we owned, I maintained, and he played,
the keys—that looked inert and motionless— were always
 slightly quivering.
They were in perfect balance when most *apt*
to rise or fall, like wings.

Between us grew a deep pact that we had begun (wordlessly)
during a trip to Canada. Where we spent an entire day without eating,
bent over obsolete pianos, studying their action geometries.

Affirming that a side effect can survive
without ever becoming useful.

We lived together for 14 years and during that time I estimated that he
misunderstood what I said 60% of the time, not from deafness—
then understood my explanation almost 100%.

A side effect of his years of music was to know precisely
how a composition should sound in performance.
But he preferred to play instead of practicing.

I wanted to write the best poetry possible, not the
best I was capable of. This came to involve, now and then,

a kind of levitation, starting with my shoes
lifting me 1/8" or so above the floor.
And to somehow have earned this skill—was it?

What consumed me in later days was the way poetry
can be—actually must be, if at all—a spiritual practice.
I could feel myself slowly relinquishing my public history,
which is to say, the story of myself, over this issue.

But he pretended not to notice, and I didn't believe him, which is
what we both needed.

His love of music was the glass
he understood through darkly—it was the only way he knew.

Once when he was driving slowly down a country road,
and I was looking out the window, I called out "Stop!"
Because I expected to see an owl sitting on a bush,
directly opposite the open window,
exactly as I had once seen years ago
on the other side of the country.

Whether the owl was there or not,
this was tip of our iceberg—not because
he loved owls above other birds, but because
his love would always return to me that way, gratuitously.

He was affectionate, and I thought I was too, at first,
but it turned out
I was changing-over the whole time, to some kind of opposite
that still allows love. He was willing to wait.

The Psychoanalysis of House-Love

Especially tomorrow mustn't find out where I am—
    —O. V. de L. Milosz, *Fourteen Poems*

I am looking for the keys to a house not mine.
Is this what happens after three days of seeing faces in everything?
Three days of a rain that revealed every rock and shrub in this city
to have a sharp nose in profile, squashed rooty mouth, elaborate ears
like wrought iron piano keys, eyes streaked by rivulets of
    smashed stars.

                                    And on the fourth day, languidly,
seeking relief in something that would have no face,
I lifted my eyes to a homely, awkward and elderly white house
mute on a loud street.

I have passed this house week after week during my lifetime in
    this city,
but never looked through its hedges.

Inside a single second, the house reminded me
it is possible to live *instead*,

    brushing tangles of desiccated bougainvillea
    from a dusty attic window
    making comfort for a house's latter years.
Already I am downstairs on the landing by the front door
looking for my keys—yes, there must be more than one.

"A passing fancy!" someone might be saying, who knows nothing
    of the protracted kinetics of stones, of how dry leaves
    encounter flagstones
each year at the end of summer, how the shapes blend and swirl,

taking the eyes gently out of focus
and letting the throat open—that the fricative airs of late
    summer drought
may sow their small abrasions throughout the body: imitating
    childen's
voices, imitating rain.

Letting me believe
that for whatever beauty I have left to lavish
there is a peculiar mystery it may serve.

Auntie Dwendy and the Toast Butterer's Apprentice

In their country yellow
drains from the sky well before sunset
every day of the year. Most afternoons
he drops his butter knife into the East River
and the two of them
hump their gear onto donkeys' backs
to head out for more rural pickings.

Past the mounds and furrows, the spinning sods
the scorched stones, the final gash of golden
into the Colorless Lands, where in wind-plagued
villages, after the clearcuts, peasants have learned
to slather their bread with Opuntia basilaris
not with oil.

Attentive to the thermodynamics of morning toast
the aspiring maestro wields his tool
only at breakfast's affluent tables, his gestures fluid
as those of a conductor's wand.

Afternoons, as he wanes, she
offers him—to replace his knife—
a handful of thorns.

Who is this butterfly?
Prick him
and he does not cry. Among constants he
is the variable of choice, his tin woodman heart
blazes not, lies as a honey Scylla in his chest.

By twilight she's a husk, and he
a dark semi-circle atop his nag,
as together they ply
the ebb and flow of forests
under the ancient wisdom of the flames.

Occiput

twice I have fallen backwards
                                                                         first on ice

the sound really was "Bonk!" (capitalized)
    echoing a bit

        but only from within

the way "witch eh tee" (thrice) spells a yellowthroat's song
not an owl snoring   which
        I never heard
        can't imitate but
        would recognize

leading me to dismiss
        lasting damage to the memory circuits
so I got up and kept walking home.

                                            Second while climbing stairs
    after sitting in the sun with wine
    three days after you died

                         left out the bottom step

the back of the head shaped as an overhanging cliff
concave
hollowed out
can be cradled   in the hands   of the occupant

no longer able to tell
        in some fashion
            still
                      honey from air

An Instance of the Feather

The way up is the way back
        —Heraclitus

All through July
blue feathers of the Scrub Jay
have surfaced
at the rate of one per day throughout my garden.
Strewn! I might have said last year,
as if they drifted from the trees,
but that was months before the plague,
and only weeks before the fires.

I can see, though, even while they are green,
how leaves resemble feathers, and wonder
how recently they turned
away from bone.

Is perhaps
something that was once
a bird
        stirring?

In Greece one summer, among archaeology volunteers,
I walked the olive orchards near Pylos
scanning the ground for pottery shards
still surfacing
from one of the lesser palaces of Nestor,

        while the olive farmers
turned off their pesticide machines for a week,
and prayed for us to fail.

Canyon Wren

It being February, even in southern New Mexico the shadows
never left —morning ones overlapping the early infiltrations
of afternoon and what's more

along our hiking trail (a gravel riverbed) the landscape seemed
to color these shadows with pastels
before they could clot and brood, and the clouds

sweeping across the surrounding hills and distant higher peaks
were more like bruises at the edge of a terrain
of edges, no hollows here to suck me into claustrophobic reveries.

Later, in the photos we took of one another I can see a second,
gamin spirit looking out from behind our faces
as if we were being reminded not to overstay our time.

Mornings we drove 20 miles to an IHOP that mercifully offered
bacon & eggs to get us to the more distant canyons where
on the third day we hoped to find the canyon wren.

At the top of the final—in the park brochure "stone stairway" —
recovering our equilibrium, we ambled along a wide corridor of leaves
from small trees, a creek nearby.

We talked fondly of wrens, their tummy shape,
the way they commit their entire bodies when they sing,
almost falling off the branch, and then

the path took a sharp right turn and closed in like a London street
in Shakespeare's time, its floor uneven, cobbled, slanting slightly
downward. Except for brown, the colors suddenly withdrew.

❋

From everything—the sky, from the vines drying on the canyon
    wall, from
our clothes, our skin, our hearts: you busied yourself with
    photos, took one of me
standing halfway up the side of the tilted cliff without knowing how
I got there. We looked again down the canyon's zig-zag throat,
    decided

to turn around, and a small, comic wren, appeared,
bustling at the bottom of a sprawling prickly pear.
I sat down, you vanished.

Indifferently, the day disgorged a couple of extra hours, so that

we woke up wondering how long had we been hearing the bird sing
while we were not listening because the sound was so much like
    water or stone
already there, sharply small in its fulsome descent.

Hinge

August rests itself, hay-colored and inert upon the yard.
The setting sun, a serpent's tongue across the desiccated grass
strikes horizontal
against the sunflowers in the raised bed, most of them
facing the wrong direction
for their own good reason.

                                              Reminds me of yesterday
the photos
on the wall of the eye doctor's room
the black holes in the exact center
of rayed orange circles—how the eye resembles
      (when photographed thus)—a sunflower
           whose pupil, dark with seed-threads,

will contract to avoid blinding.

I jump into the hinge of light leaning open
against the Japanese maple's trunk.

This is where laughter resides,
its mansion of fireflies.

The Piano Dreamed

The piano dreamed she had fingernails
which was odd because how could she
prefer their narrow lacquered surfaces to
the plastic she was born with —
                      and heaving herself around
like an elephant trying to see its tail,
she fuddled back through two centuries of forbidden ivories
to feel the smooth pulse of wooden keys
still glowing with life.

Much in the same way I long for
things to be still here
after I've forgotten them so deeply
that I no longer know if I'm fabricating histories
that did not actually exist.

I remember a braided rug I wove
while I was waiting for my second boy
to be born, out of old blankets, a wool skirt
I rarely wore, and how it was blue near
the middle, but green in the very center.
We put it on the floor for him
to lie on, but it never would stay totally
flat. Did I think of it then as a small sea,
prone to squalls?

And there's that fence where four donkeys,
unable to see over it, brayed together
in the mornings. Remember
how their loud and rhythmic
screeches tried to kindle our desperation?
But there was no way to stop ourselves
from laughing every time.

Another Reason

The sky is always dark blue, trending towards lavender
when I remember and say—*we should not go extinct,*
and each time this knowledge arrives
like a silent taxi headlamp in the rain.

This evening it comes in a black and white video
of Grigory Sokolov playing a Bach Partita,
his soft white hair shining out of the preponderant dark
as he hunches over the piano keys,
his hands up and down, one after another,
each like a falcon rising
through its precisely hollowed wind
then falling, falling to its prey.
His rounded shoulders
enact the geometry he long ago committed to
in secret prayer. The odd, old
bulk of him, the sweet mild eyebrows,
speak of books and candles;
but here is the orchard again (with its dark blue scent
of rain and lavender) coming up so close beside the house.

The Robin's Temporary

At the end of my driveway the silhouette of a robin
hops across the gravel gap between forsythia and rose.

Later
in early dusk she will sing and I again
will steady myself for being taken hostage
by a series of short musical phrases that
                                        do not
move towards or away from
meaningful words.

Deftly invisible, the voice
      sets a small round glass table
      into place on the gravel
      to reflect like the strange eyes of a cat,
      something overhead.

Tonight
the robin sings of silver and water. I hear
a long-ago sword fight in the back streets
of Venice
                that laps at the edges
                    of a sparser story, somewhat more obscure, and

all of it told
from the underside of the pearled droplet of the third segment
of her purl

by a process none of us has ever stopped to recognize.
                                                Not hope exactly,
but a way in and out, steady glimmer
of how it would feel to need-not-know just now —
a future. The Robin's song will cover all possibilities
relentlessly. Wait her out.

About the Author

Anita Sullivan is a poet, essayist, and novelist who lives in Oregon's Willamette Valley. She has previously published four essay collections, a novel, two poetry chapbooks, and a full-length poetry collection. She was a founding member of the poetry publishing collective in Portland, Oregon, called Airlie Press. Her first collection of essays *The Seventh Dragon: The Riddle of Equal Temperament*, won the Western States Book Award for creative nonfiction, and a second essay collection, *The Rhythm Of It: Poetry's Hidden Dance* (Shanti Arts, 2019) was a finalist for the Montaigne Medal in conjunction with the Eric Hoffer Book Award.

—www.anitasullivan.org

Shanti Arts

Nature • Art • Spirit

Please visit us online
to browse our entire book catalog,
including poetry collections and fiction,
books on travel, nature, healing, art,
photography, and more.

Also take a look at our highly regarded art
and literary journal, *Still Point Arts Quarterly*,
which may be downloaded for free.

www.shantiarts.com

CPSIA information can be obtained
at www.ICGtesting.com
Printed in the USA
BVHW031113281022
650563BV00014B/1351